Human Factors in Airport Surface Incidents: An Analysis of Pilot Reports Submitted to the Aviation Safety Reporting System (ASRS)

DOT/FAA/AR-06/5
DOT-VNTSC-FAA-06-14

Office of Runway Safety
& Operational Services
Washington, D.C. 20024

Amanda DiFiore
Kim Cardosi, Ph.D.

U.S. Department of Transportation
Research and Innovative Technology Administration
John A. Volpe National Transportation Systems Center
Cambridge, MA 02142-1093

Final Report
December 2006

U.S. Department of Transportation
Federal Aviation Administration

REPORT DOCUMENTATION PAGE

Form Approved
OMB No. 0704-0188

Public reporting burden for this collection of information is estimated to average 1 hour per response, including the time for reviewing instructions, searching existing data sources, gathering and maintaining the data needed, and completing and reviewing the collection of information. Send comments regarding this burden estimate or any other aspect of this collection of information, including suggestions for reducing this burden, to Washington Headquarters Services, Directorate for Information Operations and Reports, 1215 Jefferson Davis Highway, Suite 1204, Arlington, VA 22202-4302, and to the Office of Management and Budget, Paperwork Reduction Project (0704-0188), Washington, DC 20503.

1. AGENCY USE ONLY (Leave blank)	2. REPORT DATE December 2006	3. REPORT TYPE AND DATES COVERED Final report May 2004 – January 2005

4. TITLE AND SUBTITLE Human Factors in Airport Surface Incidents: An Analysis of Pilot Reports Submitted to the Aviation Safety Reporting System (ASRS)	5. FUNDING NUMBERS FA6A/DD275
6. AUTHOR(S) Amanda DiFiore and Kim Cardosi	

7. PERFORMING ORGANIZATION NAME(S) AND ADDRESS(ES) U.S. Department of Transportation Research and Innovative Technology Administration John A. Volpe National Transportation Systems Center 55 Broadway Cambridge, MA 02142-1093	8. PERFORMING ORGANIZATION REPORT NUMBER DOT-VNTSC-FAA-06-14

9. SPONSORING/MONITORING AGENCY NAME(S) AND ADDRESS(ES) Federal Aviation Administration Office of Runway Safety & Operational Services Washington, DC 20024	10. SPONSORING/MONITORING AGENCY REPORT NUMBER DOT/FAA/AR-06/5

11. SUPPLEMENTARY NOTES

12a. DISTRIBUTION/AVAILABILITY STATEMENT This document is available to the public through the National Technical Information Service, Springfield, Virginia 22161.	12b. DISTRIBUTION CODE

13. ABSTRACT (Maximum 200 words)

The purpose of this study was to examine human factors involved in airport surface incidents as reported by pilots. Reports submitted to the Aviation Safety Reporting System (ASRS) are a good source of information regarding the human performance issues and/or failures that contribute to surface incidents and can be used to supplement the information contained in FAA reports of pilot deviations. This study examined 300 ASRS reports of airport surface movement events (runway incursions and surface incidents) at the 34 busiest towered airports in the U.S., submitted between May 2001 and August 2002. The reports were selected to include those filed by a captain or first officer who was operating the aircraft under FAA Part 121, 135, or 91, and who was directly involved in the incident.

14. SUBJECT TERMS Aviation System Reporting System, runway incursions, pilot error, human factors, surface incidents, pilot-controller communication errors, runway safety	15. NUMBER OF PAGES 32
	16. PRICE CODE

17. SECURITY CLASSIFICATION OF REPORT Unclassified	18. SECURITY CLASSIFICATION OF THIS PAGE Unclassified	19. SECURITY CLASSIFICATION OF ABSTRACT Unclassified	20. LIMITATION OF ABSTRACT

NSN 7540-01-280-5500

Standard Form 298 (Rev. 2-89)
Prescribed by ANSI Std. 239-18
298-102

i

METRIC/ENGLISH CONVERSION FACTORS

ENGLISH TO METRIC

LENGTH (APPROXIMATE)

1 inch (in) = 2.5 centimeters (cm)
1 foot (ft) = 30 centimeters (cm)
1 yard (yd) = 0.9 meter (m)
1 mile (mi) = 1.6 kilometers (km)

AREA (APPROXIMATE)

1 square inch (sq in, in^2) = 6.5 square centimeters (cm^2)
1 square foot (sq ft, ft^2) = 0.09 square meter (m^2)
1 square yard (sq yd, yd^2) = 0.8 square meter (m^2)
1 square mile (sq mi, mi^2) = 2.6 square kilometers (km^2)
1 acre = 0.4 hectare (he) = 4,000 square meters (m^2)

MASS - WEIGHT (APPROXIMATE)

1 ounce (oz) = 28 grams (gm)
1 pound (lb) = 0.45 kilogram (kg)
1 short ton = 2,000 pounds (lb) = 0.9 tonne (t)

VOLUME (APPROXIMATE)

1 teaspoon (tsp) = 5 milliliters (ml)
1 tablespoon (tbsp) = 15 milliliters (ml)
1 fluid ounce (fl oz) = 30 milliliters (ml)
1 cup (c) = 0.24 liter (l)
1 pint (pt) = 0.47 liter (l)
1 quart (qt) = 0.96 liter (l)
1 gallon (gal) = 3.8 liters (l)
1 cubic foot (cu ft, ft^3) = 0.03 cubic meter (m^3)
1 cubic yard (cu yd, yd^3) = 0.76 cubic meter (m^3)

TEMPERATURE (EXACT)

[(x-32)(5/9)] °F = y °C

METRIC TO ENGLISH

LENGTH (APPROXIMATE)

1 millimeter (mm) = 0.04 inch (in)
1 centimeter (cm) = 0.4 inch (in)
1 meter (m) = 3.3 feet (ft)
1 meter (m) = 1.1 yards (yd)
1 kilometer (km) = 0.6 mile (mi)

AREA (APPROXIMATE)

1 square centimeter (cm^2) = 0.16 square inch (sq in, in^2)
1 square meter (m^2) = 1.2 square yards (sq yd, yd^2)
1 square kilometer (km^2) = 0.4 square mile (sq mi, mi^2)
10,000 square meters (m^2) = 1 hectare (ha) = 2.5 acres

MASS - WEIGHT (APPROXIMATE)

1 gram (gm) = 0.036 ounce (oz)
1 kilogram (kg) = 2.2 pounds (lb)
1 tonne (t) = 1,000 kilograms (kg) = 1.1 short tons

VOLUME (APPROXIMATE)

1 milliliter (ml) = 0.03 fluid ounce (fl oz)
1 liter (l) = 2.1 pints (pt)
1 liter (l) = 1.06 quarts (qt)
1 liter (l) = 0.26 gallon (gal)

1 cubic meter (m^3) = 36 cubic feet (cu ft, ft^3)
1 cubic meter (m^3) = 1.3 cubic yards (cu yd, yd^3)

TEMPERATURE (EXACT)

[(9/5) y + 32] °C = x °F

QUICK INCH - CENTIMETER LENGTH CONVERSION

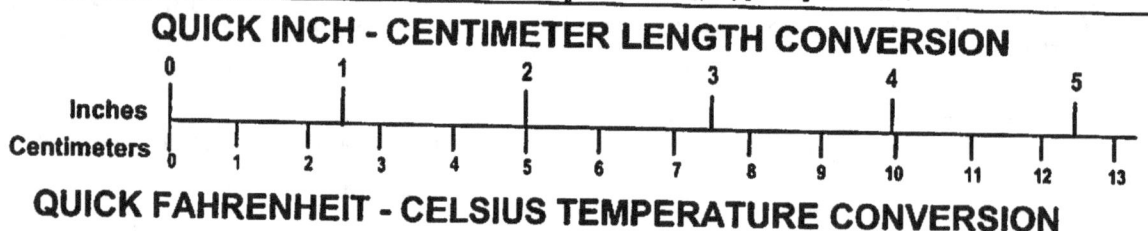

QUICK FAHRENHEIT - CELSIUS TEMPERATURE CONVERSION

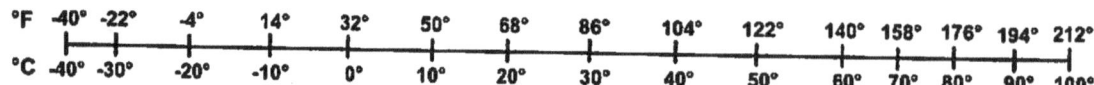

For more exact and or other conversion factors, see NIST Miscellaneous Publication 286, Units of Weights and Measures. Price $2.50 SD Catalog No. C13 10286

Updated 6/17/98

Preface

The Federal Aviation Administration's Office of Runway Safety and Operational Services sponsored this research. We would like to extend our appreciation to the analysts at the Battelle — Aviation Safety Reporting System (ASRS) office who performed the searches for the relevant ASRS reports.

Table of Contents

List of Figures

Executive Summary

The purpose of this study was to examine human and other contributing factors involved in airport surface incidents as reported by pilots. Reports submitted to the Aviation Safety Reporting System (ASRS) are a good source of information regarding human performance issues and/or failures that contribute to surface incidents and can be used to supplement the information contained in FAA reports of pilot deviations. One method of identifying human factors involved in surface events is to examine those reports submitted by individuals who were directly involved in an incident.

This study examined 300 ASRS reports of airport surface movement events (i.e., runway incursions and surface incidents) at the 34 busiest airports in the United States, submitted between May 2001 and August 2002. The reports selected for inclusion were those filed by a captain or first officer who was operating the aircraft under FAA Part 121, 135, or 91, and who was directly involved in the incident. Of the 300 sampled reports, 50 were excluded because they failed to meet study criteria (e.g., described an error of a pilot in another aircraft). Of the remaining reports, 14 percent were filed by pilots and co-pilots describing the same incident; the information from these duplicate reports was combined yielding 231 unique incidents.

Reports were divided into the following six categories of outcomes of surface incidents: crossing the hold-short lines, entering the runway, completely crossing the runway, taxiing into position and holding (TIPH), taking off, and landing. The number of reports involving takeoffs without authorization or landings without authorization were insufficient to analyze the contributing factors. Contributing factors of surface incidents were grouped into six basic categories: communication factors; airport surface issues; position awareness; automatic processing factors; environmental factors; and other human performance issues. Factors from the latter two categories were not cited often in this sample of reports and thus were not examined in detail. Each of the four remaining high-level categories contained specific factors that were analyzed individually. For example, readback errors were analyzed separately and were subsumed under the category of "communications."

Crossing the Hold-short Line

Thirty-five percent of the ASRS reports involved incidents in which pilots crossed the hold-short lines without authorization. This statistic mirrors the frequency of these incidents found in runway incursion data. In 2004, one-quarter of pilot deviations resulting in runway incursions involved crossing the hold-short lines (but not the runway edge) without authorization. Surprisingly, almost 40 percent of these pilot errors reported to the FAA included a correct readback of the "hold-short" instruction (FAA, 2005). Among the ASRS reports where a pilot crossed the hold-short lines without authorization, more than 40 percent of the pilots reported a loss of "position awareness"; that is, they intended to hold short, and crossed the hold-short lines without realizing it. In such cases, crossing the hold-short lines without authorization was most often related to the pilot performing heads-down tasks. In fact, in 26 percent of these incidents, the pilot reported being heads down in the cockpit either performing checklists or programming flight deck systems as they crossed the hold-short lines.

In one-third of the reports involving a pilot erroneously crossing the hold-short lines, expectations or reverting to habit contributed to the incident. For example, pilots frequently mentioned that either the hold lines were not where they expected them to be or that they were accustomed to taking a certain route to the assigned runway (and thus, holding at a different location than instructed). When the instructions differed from what was expected, pilots unintentionally reverted to habit. In addition, some pilots reported simply following the aircraft in front of them across the hold lines, even though they intended to hold short.

Entering and Crossing the Runway

This analysis of ASRS reports showed that loss of position awareness is the number one factor in pilots *entering* and *crossing* a runway without authorization. In 2004, 40 percent of pilot deviations that resulted in runway incursions involved pilots entering the runway. An additional 35 percent involved pilots completely crossing the runway. In approximately 35 percent of these instances, there was another aircraft taking off; in approximately 65 percent, there was another aircraft landing. While most of the landing aircraft went around, less than one-quarter of the takeoffs resulted in an aborted takeoff.

Again, the analysis of ASRS reports revealed that the most common contributing factor to these types of errors was the pilot being heads down. One-third of the pilots who crossed or entered the runway without authorization reported that one of the pilots was head-down at the time of the incident, most often performing a checklist.

Another coincident factor to crossing the runway without authorization was the use of "taxi to" instructions. Pilots did not report any confusion regarding the controller's intent of the "taxi to" instruction, but an error in position awareness, combined with the clearance to cross intervening runways, resulted in the pilot crossing a runway without a clearance. For example, in some cases pilots took a wrong turn and ended up crossing a runway that they wouldn't have crossed if they had taken the correct route. In other cases, the aircraft was not where the controller thought it was. The clearance to "taxi to" allowed an aircraft to cross a runway that the controller did not intend the aircraft to cross.

Taxi Into Position and Hold (TIPH)

In 2004, 9 percent of pilot deviations (resulting in a runway incursion) involved an aircraft that entered the runway without clearance and held in position awaiting authorization for takeoff. ASRS reports revealed that this type of error is almost always due to communication errors. Ninety-four percent of Taxi Into Position and Hold (TIPH) reports cited communication issues as directly contributing to the incident. The most commonly cited communication factors were readback/hearback errors, accepting another aircraft's clearance, frequency congestion, and blocked communications.

Recommendations

The following recommendations are offered for reducing surface incidents caused by pilot deviations:

- Minimize pilots' heads-down time for the purpose of maintaining position awareness.

- Continue to analyze the risk inherent in "taxi to" instructions.

- Reduce blocked transmissions and frequency congestion.

- Augment pilot's expectation of the "hold-short" lines.

- Continue to maintain improvements in airport signs and markings in order to promote position awareness.

1. Introduction

1.1 Background

The Federal Aviation Administration (FAA) attributes runway incursions to pilot error (pilot deviations), air traffic controller error (operational errors), or the error of a vehicle driver or pedestrian (vehicle/pedestrian deviations). To determine the factors that pilots perceive as contributing to surface incidents, reports submitted to the Aviation Safety Reporting System (ASRS) were examined. The ASRS is a catalog of reports of events that, in the reporter's opinion, affected the safety of flight. Most ASRS reports are submitted by pilots. Self-reports of errors present a candid portrayal of human performance issues that the person may or may not wish to relay to an investigative authority.

ASRS reports are filed on a voluntary basis; however, as an incentive to report, pilots who incur a deviation are given limited immunity from disciplinary action if they choose to file a report. ASRS reports are limited in the sense that they represent subjective opinions and are not independently verified by an objective party. In addition, one cannot assume that the frequency of occurrence in ASRS reports represents the actual frequency of occurrence in day-to-day operations. Despite the inherent limitations of the ASRS, these reports provide a wealth of information on the factors involved in pilot deviations. The goal of this analysis was to identify human factors that pilots perceive as contributing to surface incidents.

1.2 Report Selection

Three hundred of the most recent ASRS reports of airport surface movement events involving human performance issues were sampled from the 34 busiest airports in the United States (see Figure 1). The most recent reports available were those submitted between May 2001 and August 2002.

Criteria for inclusion in this analysis were two-fold. First, the incident had to meet the FAA requirements to be classified as a surface incident involving runway operations. The FAA defines a surface event as:

> "Any event where unauthorized or unapproved movement occurs
> within the movement area, or an occurrence in the movement area
> associated with the operation of an aircraft that affects or could
> affect the safety of flight. A surface incident can occur anywhere
> on the airport's surface, including the runway." -- FAA Runway
> Safety Report, 2005

The FAA further classifies surface incidents as runway incursions and non-runway incursions. This analysis examines only surface incidents involving runway operations but includes incidents that both involved and did not involve other aircraft; i.e., the analysis includes both incursion and non-incursion ("surface incident") events.

1

Second, a pilot, or a co-pilot, who was operating the aircraft under FAA Part 121, 135, or 91 and was directly involved in the incident, must have filed the report. Of the 300 sampled reports, 50 were excluded for one or more of the following reasons: (1) the reporting pilot was reporting the error of a pilot in another aircraft, (2) there was not enough information in the narrative to code the report with respect to human factors, (3) the report was filed by a controller, or (4) the primary cause of the incident was attributed to equipment or other issues unrelated to human factors.

Of the 250 reports included in the analysis, 14 percent were filed by pilots and co-pilots describing the same incident; information from these duplicate reports was combined. For most of these reports, pilots generally cited the same factors. To avoid inflating the frequency of occurrence of factors from these duplicate reports, factors identified by both the pilot and co-pilot were only counted once. Often, however, pilots would cite additional factors that their co-pilot failed to cite. These factors were also included in the analysis. As a result of combining the data from duplicate reports, a total of 231 unique incidents were analyzed.

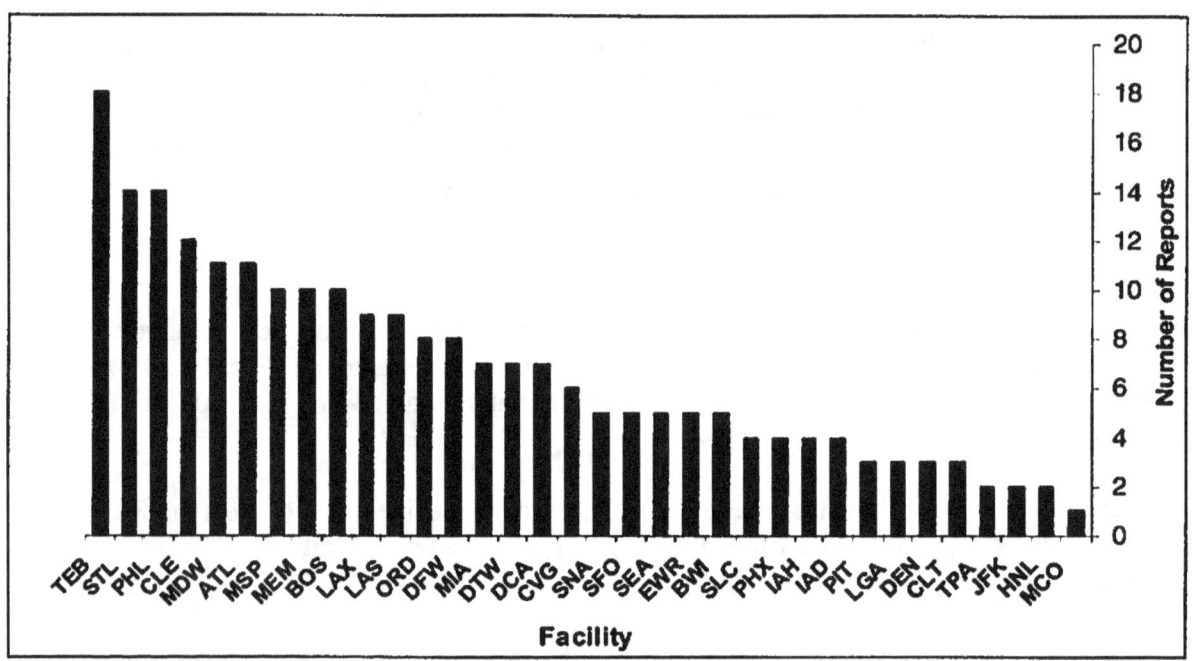

Figure 1. Number of ASRS reports analyzed from each airport in order of decreasing frequency.

1.3 Report Characteristics

Figure 1 shows the distribution of reports analyzed in this analysis by the airport where they occurred (the airports are identified by their three-letter identifier in Appendix A). While this information is of general interest, it is important to note that the frequency of reports submitted does not reflect the occurrence of runway incursions for two reasons. First, the events reported to ASRS could have been classified either as runway incursions or surface incidents. Second, as previously mentioned, reports submitted to ASRS do not reflect the actual occurrence in day-to-day operations.

Type of Operation. As can be seen in Figure 2, the majority of reports were filed by pilots operating under Commercial rules (Part 121 or Part 135). A separate analysis comparing reports filed by pilots operating under Commercial rules (121/135) and General Aviation rules (91) revealed no remarkable differences in the type of incidents or factors these pilots cited.

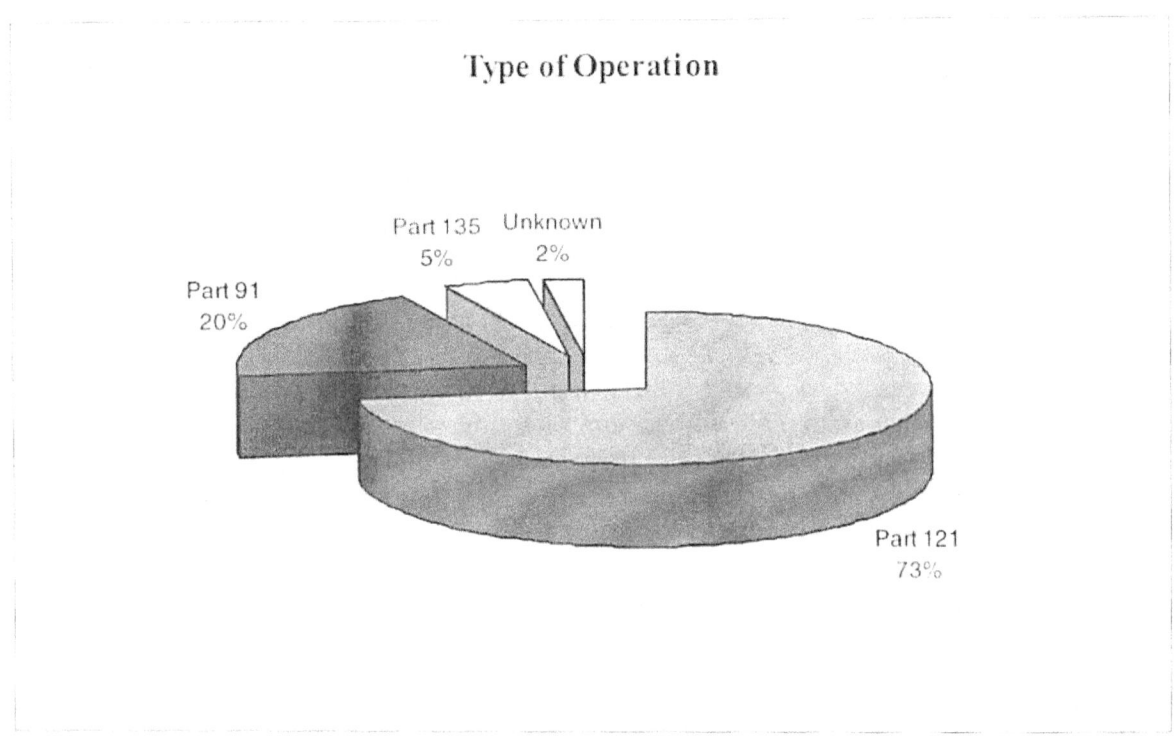

Figure 2. Percentage of ASRS reports analyzed by type of operation.

Crew Size. Eighty-seven percent of the reports examined involved two-person crews and 5 percent involved a three-person crew. Only 7 percent of the reports analyzed involved a single-person crew. Crew-size was not identified in 1 percent of the reports.

Involvement of Other Aircraft and Avoidance Maneuvers. Less than half (44 percent) of the reports involved another aircraft. When another aircraft was involved, 50 percent of the reports described the execution of an avoidance maneuver. The most common avoidance maneuver (in 80 percent of these cases) was a go-around or the execution of a missed approach.

Relative Location. The majority of the incidents (66 percent) occurred at the intersection of a runway and a taxiway. These incidents included those in which an aircraft crossed the hold-short lines without authorization (but did not cross the runway edge) with another aircraft on the runway. An additional 10 percent occurred at an intersection of two runways. The remaining 24 percent occurred on a single runway (e.g., involving two aircraft on, or almost on, the same runway at the same time).

1.4 Categorization of Human Factors

Each report was examined to identify the involvement of factors contributing to human performance errors. The analysis identified specific factors that can be grouped into the following categories:

1. *Communication Factors* - miscommunications between pilots and controllers as a result of a communication error (such as a readback error) and as a result of a misunderstanding of ATC instruction. Communication Factors also included issues such as frequency congestion, blocked transmissions, partially blocked transmissions, and quality of radio transmission.

2. *Airport Surface Issues* - signage, markings, and complexities associated with complex airport geometry.

3. *Position Awareness* - factors associated with the pilot's ability to correctly identify his or her location on the airport surface and anticipate an approaching runway.

4. *Automatic Processing Factors* - actions that occurred out of habit, usually as a result of extensive experience and often without conscious awareness. For example, if a pilot is accustomed to a particular taxi route and is given a route that is slightly different, the pilot may unintentionally revert to the more familiar route even though the actual clearance was understood.

5. *Environmental Factors* - factors related to weather or visibility such as day/night and icy or wet surface conditions affecting human performance.

6. *Other Human Performance Issues* - fatigue, distraction, and being rushed.

Appendix B contains the complete taxonomy of specific factors.

2. Results and Analysis

2.1 Human Factors

Factors by Category. As can be seen in Figure 3, communications were the most frequently reported factor category, cited in more than half (55 percent) of all the reports examined. Inadequate position awareness was the second most common category, cited in 40 percent of all reports. Automatic processing and airport surface issues were each cited in approximately one-quarter of the reports (25 percent and 23 percent, respectively). Less frequently cited factors were other human performance factors (fatigue, distraction, and being rushed, 20 percent); and environmental factors (18 percent).

Only 10 percent of the reports identified weather as a contributing factor. Seventy-five percent of the 231 incidents occurred during Visual Meteorological Conditions (VMC). Ten percent of the reports listed the conditions as Instrument Meteorological Conditions (IMC) or marginal VMC. The remainder of reports did not identify weather conditions at the time of the incident. Certain human performance issues, such as fatigue and distraction (labeled "other performance issues") and environmental factors including adverse weather conditions were the least frequently cited factor categories. While these factors are vitally important issues with respect to air traffic safety, they were cited too infrequently within this particular sample of reports to analyze, i.e., a separate analysis examining these factors, specifically, would require a larger sample of ASRS reports.

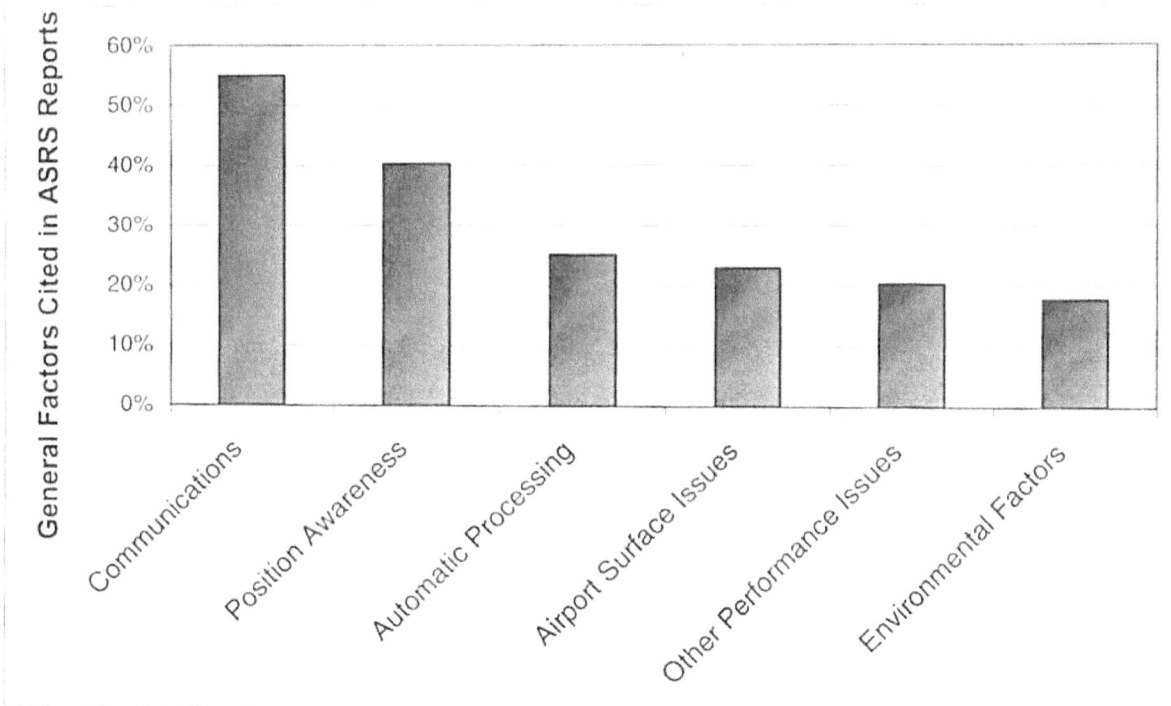

Figure 3. Human factor issues cited by pilots in ASRS reports of pilot errors that resulted in runway incursions and surface incidents.

2.2 Incident Categories

The surface incidents described in the ASRS reports were categorized into the following mutually exclusive categories of runway transgressions:

- Crossed the hold-short lines (but did not cross the runway edge);

- Entered the runway - crossed the runway edge but not to hold in position, and did not completely cross the runway.

- Taxi into position and hold (TIPH) - entered the runway to hold in position for takeoff; or

- Completely crossed the runway.

If a pilot reported that the aircraft passed the hold-short point but had not entered the runway (regardless of intent), the incident was classified as a "hold-short" incident. Crossing the hold-short lines (but not crossing the runway edge) was the most frequently described incident — occurring in 35 percent of the reports examined. Completely crossing the runway was described in 27 percent of the reports. Fifteen percent of the reports described pilots who taxied into position and held on the runway without authorization. An additional 10 percent of the reports described pilots who otherwise entered the runway without authorization. The remaining reports described runway transgressions involving takeoffs and landings (6 percent and 5 percent, respectively) and incidents that were too infrequent to be categorized (2 percent). Reports involving takeoffs and landings without authorization were too few to allow examination of the factors involved in these incidents.

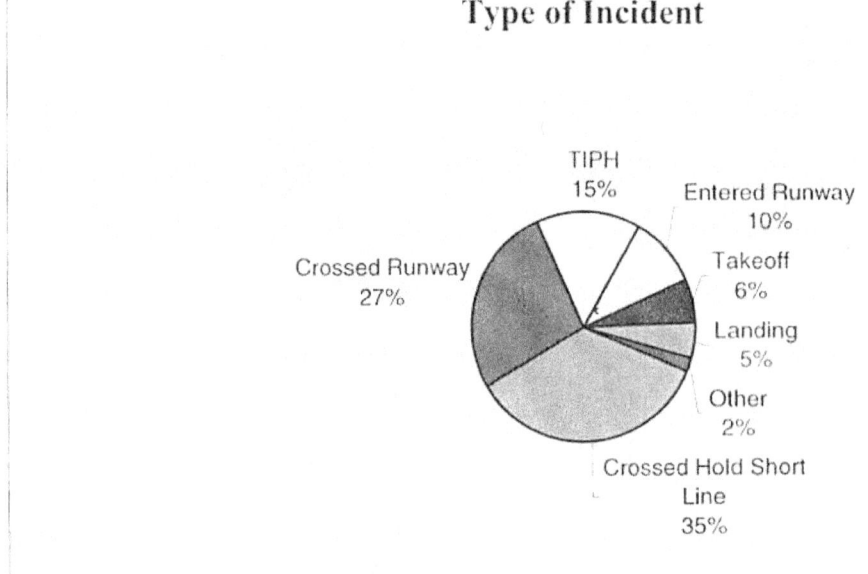

Figure 4. Distribution of incident categories.

2.3 Crossing the Hold Short Lines

Pilots' lack of awareness as to exactly where they were on the airport surface was the most common factor in reports involving crossing the hold-short lines without authorization. As can be seen in Figure 5, lack of position awareness was cited in 43 percent of reports involving a hold line incident. The most common reason for losing position awareness was engaging in "heads-down" duties, cited in 26 percent of all hold line incidents, and 60 percent of hold line incidents citing a loss of position awareness. The most frequently cited reasons for being "heads-down" were performing checklists and programming the flight management system (FMS). It is interesting to note that being heads-down was cited much more often than external factors (e.g., poor signage) in loss of position awareness that resulted in crossing the hold-short lines. The most commonly cited surface issues were complex airport geometry (22 percent) and poor or misunderstood signs and markings (16 percent).

Pilots cited communication errors and issues in one-third of all hold line incidents. This includes readback errors, controllers missing readback errors (i.e., hearback errors), misunderstanding a clearance, frequency congestion, etc. Traditional readback/hearback errors were cited in only 4 percent of hold line incidents; hearback errors where the controller failed to detect his/her own mistake in the initial instruction were cited in 1 percent of hold line incidents. Frequency and equipment issues such as poor radio quality and blocked communications were cited in a combined 6 percent of hold line incidents. It is interesting to note that no *single* communication factor was mentioned in more than 4 percent of the reports citing hold line incidents. Rather, the communication factors involved in hold line incidents were an unremarkable mix of general communication factors involved in everyday operations.

Pilot errors that occurred as the result of automatic processing or habit were cited in 31 percent of reports involving hold line incidents. The most common issue in this category was an unexpected location of the hold-short line. More than half (56 percent) of pilots citing automatic processing issues in hold line incidents reported that the hold-short line was in a nonstandard location (i.e., further away from the runway than the pilot expected).

Seventy percent of hold line incidents involved pilots taxiing for departure (as opposed to taxiing to the gate upon arrival). In other cases, the pilots were caught off-guard by the unexpected location of the hold-short lines (that is, the markings are not as close to the runway as the pilot expected). The following narrative demonstrates how the unexpected location of a hold-short line can result in an inadvertent crossing.

> "Cleared to land runway 24R at Cleveland-Hopkins following a visual approach. We were told to exit the runway at taxiway K, hold short of runway 24L for landing traffic. Due to the close spacing of the parallel runways, the hold-short line for runway 24L was right at the turnoff point at taxiway K. We rolled through that line, thinking that the next line (actually the hold-short line for runway 24R) was our hold-short point. We realized our mistake as we saw the pattern of the approaching hold-short line. Tower told us to hold our position, and runway 24L traffic landed without incident." ACN# 538577

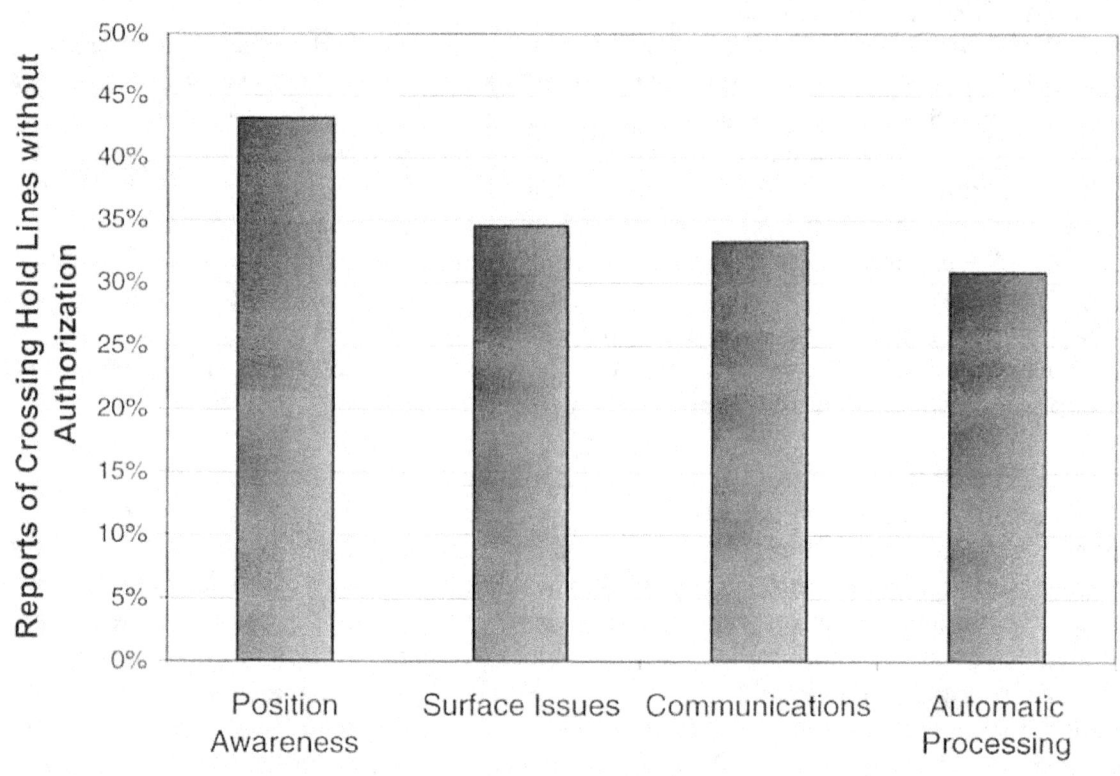

Figure 5. Factor categories in crossing the hold lines without a clearance.

2.4 Crossing the Runway Without a Clearance

The circumstances described in reports of pilots crossing the runway or taxiing into position and holding for takeoff (TIPH), are somewhat different from those of pilots crossing the hold-short lines. In these cases, pilots *intended* to take or cross a runway (but not necessarily the runway that they crossed). Pilots who crossed the runway without a clearance did so for one of two reasons. Most common was a loss of position awareness — the pilots inadvertently crossed the runway, often while one pilot was heads-down. Another common scenario included a misunderstanding involving a "taxi to" instruction; that is, the pilots misidentified their location and crossed a runway that the controller did not intend for them to cross. In both cases, the pilots were not where they thought they were at some point. The difference is that in the incidents involving "taxi to" instructions, the pilots generally *thought* they had a clearance to cross the runway that they crossed; in the other incidents, the pilots did not intend to cross the runway that they crossed. If crossing instructions had been required for all runway crossings, the outcome of the incidents involving this type of error might have been different.

As can be seen in Figure 6, the most common category of factors, cited in more than half (53 percent) of all reports involving pilots who crossed a runway without a clearance, was communications. Communication factors included readback/hearback errors (15 percent), frequency congestion and/or blocked transmissions (21 percent). The most commonly identified factor, cited in almost one-third (32 percent) of the reports describing crossing the runway without a clearance, involved "taxi to" instructions. The following example demonstrates how "taxi to" instructions resulted in an aircraft crossing the "wrong" runway due to a miscommunication regarding the location of the aircraft.

> "At TEB and FBO the first officer requested taxi from FBO (wrong FBO) to active runway. Ground controller told us to give way to a Cessna 172 and then taxi as we were not in sight by the ground controller. We did not see the C172 and asked for verification. Ground still thinks we are at another FBO. Ground tells us to taxi via taxiway L to runway 1. Taxiway L exits right in front of FBO at TEB, so now we feel she knows where we are. Taxiway L crosses runway 6/24 enroute to runway 1. We begin our taxi via taxiway L slowing to check for traffic before crossing runway 6/24. Once across runway 6/24, ground reprimands us stating that we just crossed runway 6/24 on taxiway L. Our taxi clearance was to taxi via taxiway L to runway 1 for departure, without instructions to hold short of runway 6/24. No further discussions with ground control followed. Airport ground traffic was minimal at the time and only 1 aircraft arrived before our departure. Confusion could have been avoided if we had made it more clear which FBO we were parked at." ACN# 533474

The second most commonly cited factor category in reports involving runway crossings, identified in 44 percent of the reports, was a loss of position awareness. As in reports of crossing the hold-short lines, being "heads-down" due to performing checklists or programming the FMS was the main reason for losing position awareness, cited in 32 percent of runway crossing incidents, and 74 percent of runway crossing incidents where position awareness was cited as a contributing factor. Twenty-one percent of pilots involved in runway crossing incidents simply reported misidentifying their location. The following report demonstrates how pilots are likely to cross a runway while engaging in a heads-down task such as focusing on an airport diagram or performing checklists.

> "While taxiing, [we] received instructions to follow preceding aircraft to runway 9 and hold short of runway 4L at BOS. Captain was taxiing aircraft while [the first officer was] running checklists. BOS has a bravo hold point and both captain and first officer [were distracted] by discussing proper taxi route to hold point bravo -- both first officer and captain spending a lot of time looking down at the airport diagram. Captain continued following previous aircraft across runway 4L without clearance. Ground control commented we were not cleared to cross runway 4L, but go ahead and position and hold on runway 9." ACN# 545129

Factors associated with automatic processing, such as reverting to old habit or expecting clearance to cross the runway, were cited in 27 percent of runway crossings. The most commonly cited factor was a pilot expecting a clearance to cross the runway (16 percent of runway crossings). Airport surface issues were not frequently cited in runway crossings; factors such as complex intersections or confusing signs or markings were collectively cited in only 18 percent of these reports.

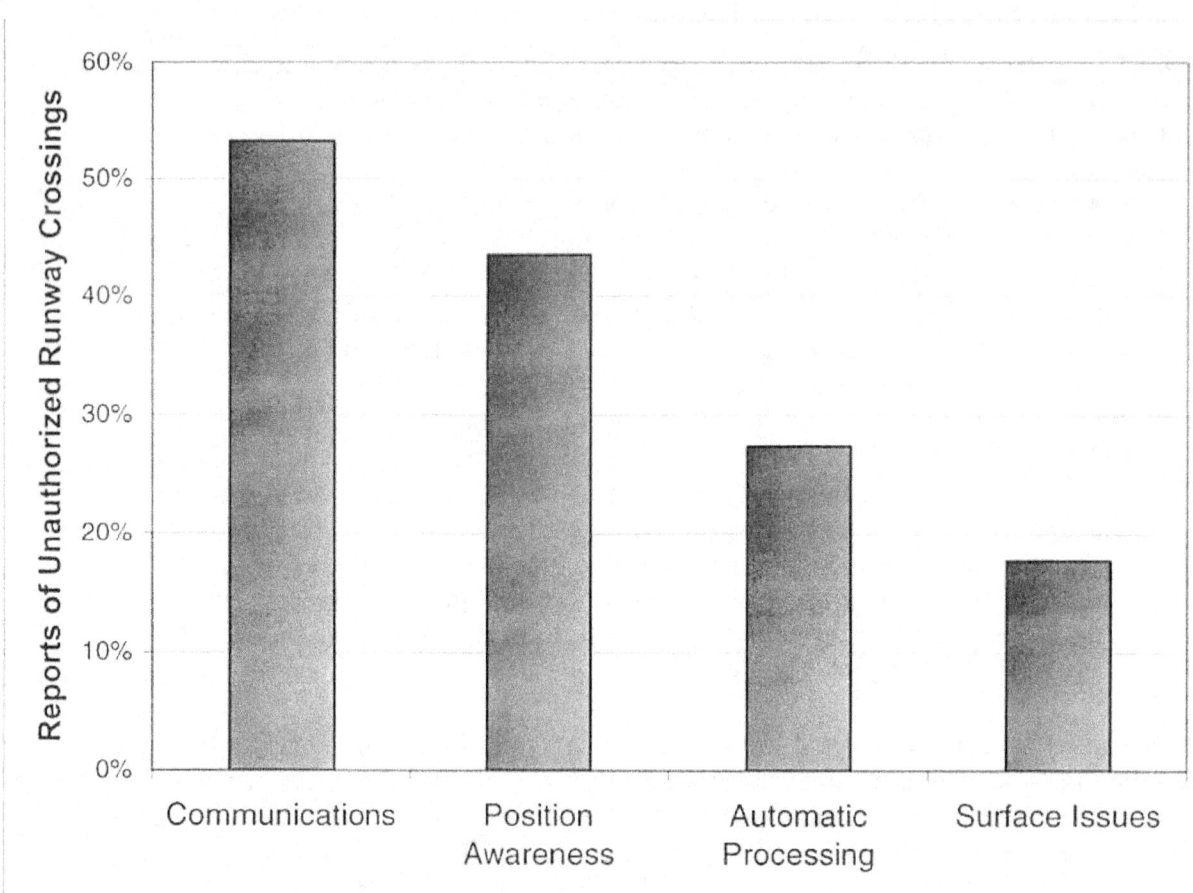

Figure 6. Factor categories cited in ASRS reports of crossing a runway without a clearance.

2.5 Taxi Into Position and Hold (TIPH) Incidents

The most likely reasons cited for pilots taxiing into position and holding on the runway (TIPH) without clearance was that the pilot expected to receive a clearance to TIPH and accepted a clearance to TIPH that was intended for another aircraft. As can be seen in Figure 7, most (94 percent) reports involving pilots taxiing onto the runway and holding (TIPH) without a clearance cited one or more of the factors in the category of communications as contributing to the incident. Readback/hearback errors were cited in 43 percent of the reports and more than one-third of the TIPH reports (34 percent) involved a pilot accepting a TIPH clearance intended for another aircraft. This parallels the finding that pilots also stated (in 26 percent of the TIPH reports) that they were expecting a TIPH clearance and they heard what they expected to hear. Frequency congestion and blocked communications were cited as a contributing factor in 29 percent of the reports. Like the reports of runway crossings, but unlike the reports in which the pilots crossed the hold-short lines, most of the pilots who taxied into position to hold on the runway *intended* to do so. Still, almost one-third of the TIPH reports mentioned that at least one member of the cockpit was performing "heads-down" duties at the time of the transgression; the most commonly cited reason for being "heads-down" was performing checklists.

Further complicating the matter was frequency congestion and blocked communications preventing the pilot from hearing the instruction in its entirety. Accepting the wrong aircraft's clearance was sometimes coincident with frequency congestion and/or blocked communications, but more often was attributable solely to the pilot's expectation of a TIPH instruction. The following narrative describes how a flight crew almost took another aircraft's clearance to TIPH on the runway most likely due to blocked communications.

> "While waiting for takeoff at DTW runway 3L, the captain and I heard clearance to taxi into position and hold by DTW tower controller. I replied back with 'taxi into position and hold runway 3L'. While taxiing toward the runway, we saw a DC9 approaching the runway from the other side. We stopped and then heard clearance from the tower for them to take off. We queried the DTW controller about our taxi into position and hold clearance. Controller replied we had no such clearance. We held our position and then were cleared for takeoff after the DC9 departed. There was no conflict. In our analysis, we suspect a communication breakdown. We think the other aircraft (DC9) and we responded at the same time when replying to taxi into position and hold, therefore, blocking out each other's radio call. We also had an ACARS WT data change during the time this miscommunication took place, adding a distraction to the situation." ACN# 534751

Another communication issue is the inconsistent use of the term "hold" in common air traffic instructions. "*Hold* short," instructs the pilot *not to enter the runway.* "Taxi into position and *hold*" instructs the pilot to *line up on the runway* and await takeoff clearance. Those two standard air traffic instructions contain similar wording to indicate opposite instructions, (i.e., get on the runway and don't get on the runway). While commonly used in Europe, the instruction to "hold your position" (meaning "stop") is nonstandard in the United States; however, it is sometimes used. Also, pilots reported that at some facilities, controllers sometimes issue the (nonstandard) instructions to "taxi up to the number one position and hold short" or "taxi full-length position and hold." The controllers' intention in each of these reports was for the pilot to hold short of the runway. However, in the incidents described, the pilots heard only "position and hold" and proceeded onto the runway. Since analysis of ASRS reports is not the same as analysis of voice tapes, one cannot say for certain that this is what the controller said. However, one can say that this is what the pilot heard (or thought he or she heard), as evidenced in the pilots' reports. The following report illustrates this point.

> "Flight XYZ holding on taxiway D short of taxiway S for runway 30L. Crew was busy getting takeoff numbers, doing taxi and before takeoff checklists. Tower transmitted 'aircraft flight XYZ, taxi up to the #1 position and hold short.' In the cockpit the 'position and hold' portion registered. We taxied onto the runway and held in position. Aircraft flight XYA had to go around. I believe that poor phraseology contributed to the incursion. Mixing 'position and hold' and 'hold short' words is confusing." ACN# 528405

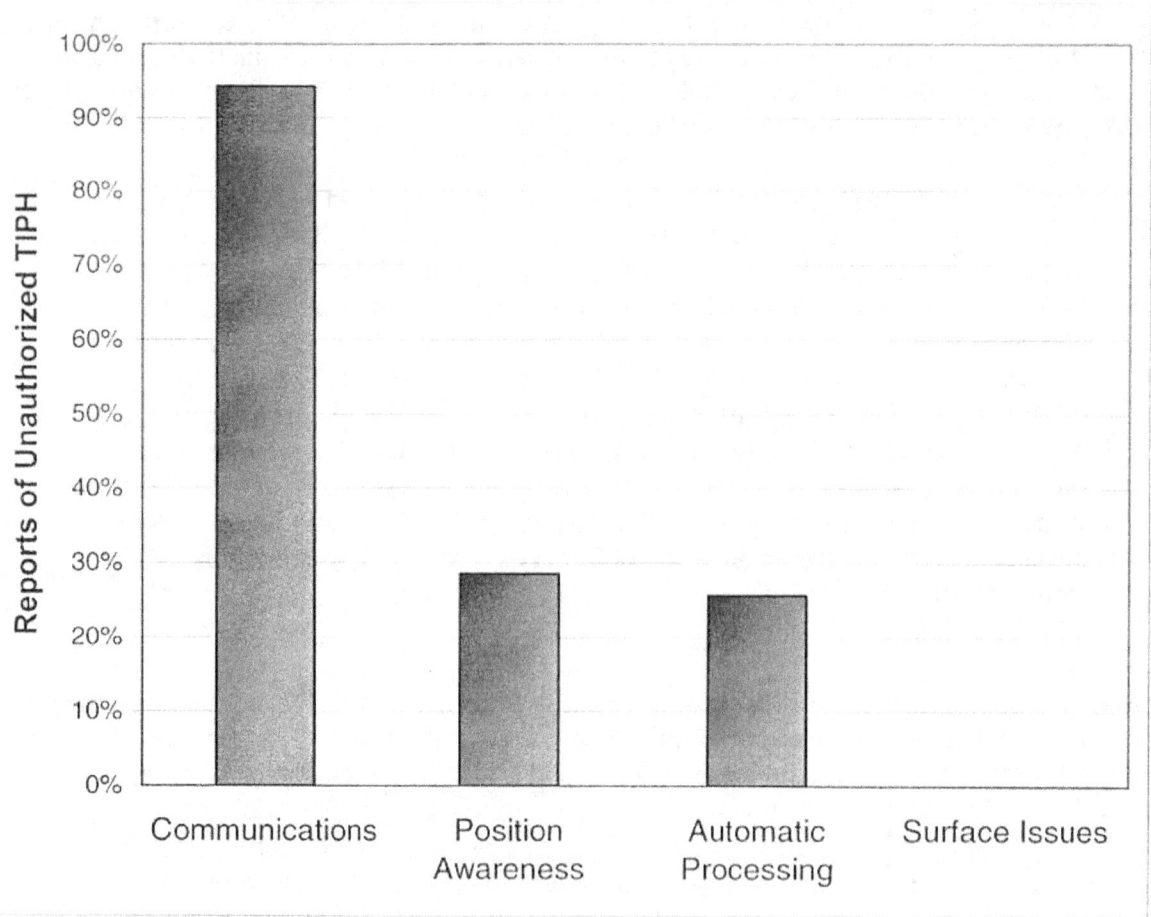

Figure 7. Factor categories cited in ASRS reports involving a pilot who taxied into position without a clearance.

2.6 Entering the Runway Without Authorization

The results of the analysis of human factors cited in reports of pilots entering the runway without authorization, that is, crossing onto the runway other than to position and hold, are very similar to the factors cited for crossing the hold-short lines, but not crossing the runway edge. **Inadequate position awareness was the predominant factor cited in these types of reports. Over half (53 percent) of the reports that cited a loss of position awareness mentioned that being "heads-down" was a contributing factor to the incident.**

General communication factors were cited in 38 percent of runway entrance incidents. The most common communication factor was incorrect ATC phraseology cited in 13 percent of runway entrance incidents. Readback/hearback errors and misunderstanding the clearance were cited in only 4 percent of the runway entrance incidents. The most commonly cited airport surface issues were poor signage and/or markings (21 percent of runway entrance incidents) and complex airport geometry (13 percent of runway entrance incidents). Pilot expectation was cited in 21 percent of reports involving runway entrance incidents; these pilots reported that they were expecting a clearance to cross the runway. In most of the reports of pilots entering the runway without authorization, the pilot started to cross the runway, realized the mistake, and stopped, or was instructed to stop by ATC.

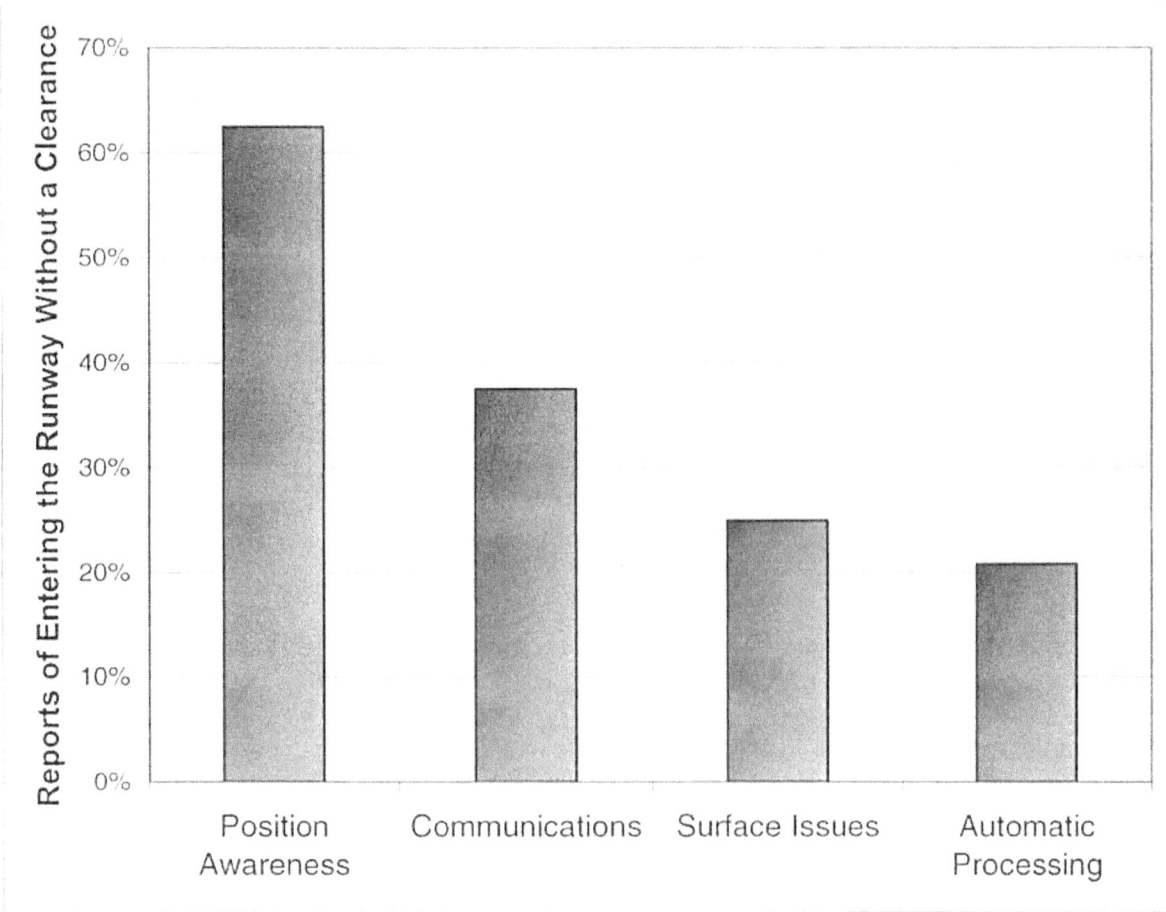

Figure 8. Types and frequencies of factors cited in ASRS reports of pilots entering the runway without authorization.

2.7 Additional Issues

Offset Taxiways. In rare cases a taxiway can be perpendicular, but not actually connect with the runway (as illustrated in Figure 9). Sometimes it is necessary for a controller to instruct a pilot to hold short of the runway in this situation (i.e., when another aircraft is landing). Pilots in this situation, particularly those not familiar with the airport, reported that they were confused as to where to hold short. Further complicating the situation were reports indicating that there was a lack of hold-short markings and/or signs at these locations. **Hold-short lines should always be located wherever the controller expects the pilot to stop.** In addition, controllers should consider informing pilots who may not be familiar with the airport that the runway does not intersect the taxiway. Pilots should always query ATC when there is ambiguity as to where to hold short of a runway.

Figure 9. Additional factor: Confusing taxiway

Blocked Transmissions and Frequency Congestion. Readback/hearback errors continue to contribute to pilot errors that result in runway transgressions. Some level of this type of human error is inevitable due to the human tendency to hear what one expects to hear. However, there are things that can be done to minimize the chances of these errors and mitigate their effects. Pilots need to ensure that all critical instructions (such as those to cross a runway, TIPH, takeoff or land) are readback with the aircraft call sign and runway designator. Controllers need to be continually vigilant with readbacks and continually monitor the aircraft to ensure that the pilot does what the controller intended them to do.

There are other changes that could be implemented to minimize communication error. Pilots often cited frequency congestion and blocked transmissions as contributing factors to readback and hearback errors. The following excerpt from a report demonstrates the extent to which frequency congestion is a problem at busy facilities.

> "As we were taxiing out, we noted there was so much congestion on the ground frequency that the ground controller was issuing clearances to aircraft and stating 'hold the readback.'" ACN# 538801

Implementation of anti-blocking technologies could help to eliminate blocked transmissions. Implementation of datalink, or other technologies that minimize the need for voice transmissions, would help to reduce frequency congestion.

Reporting Clear of the Runway. There were also a few reports from pilots of large aircraft stating the difficulty in determining whether the aircraft is completely clear of the runway when they need to hold short of a closely spaced parallel runway. Controllers and pilots need to recognize that this is a very difficult (and error-prone) task.

3. Conclusions and Recommendations

The purpose of this study was to examine human factors of surface incidents as reported by pilots. The results show that while different types of incidents had different characteristics, there were also some striking similarities. A critical difference was routed in whether the pilots *intended* to enter the runway that they transgressed. The reports of pilots who ended up crossing the hold-short lines, but not crossing the runway edge, indicated that in most cases, the pilots' *intended* to hold short of the runway. These pilots inadvertently crossed, often while one of the pilots was heads down. Similarly, pilots who *entered* the runway, other than to taxi into position and hold, also did not *intend* to enter the runway; these pilots understood the clearance, but due to a loss of position awareness, often associated with one of the pilots being heads down, inadvertently entered the runway. These and other findings of this study suggest the following recommendation:

Minimize "Heads-Down" Activity While Taxiing. Communication issues continue to contribute to human error that results in surface incidents. Pilots hearing what they expected to hear, including accepting a clearance for another aircraft was the most commonly cited factor in pilots TIPH and crossing the runway without a clearance. However, in all categories of incidents, loss of position awareness, often associated with one of the pilots being "heads down" was cited as a common contributing factor (see Figure 10).

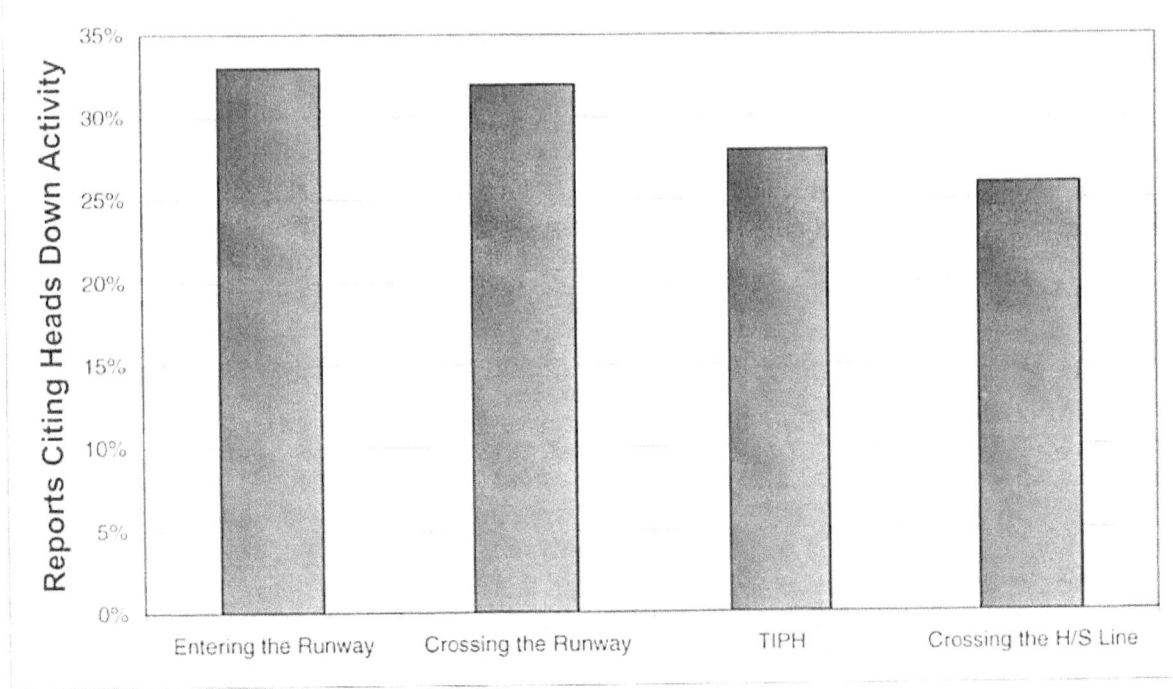

Figure 10. Percentage of ASRS reports citing "heads-down" activity as a contributing factor.

A significant finding of this study is that "heads-down" activity was associated with pilots entering, crossing, and taking the runway whether the pilots ended up crossing the hold-short lines or held on the runway for takeoff. Being "heads-down," most often for the purpose of performing checklists or programming the flight management system (FMS), was cited often as a factor in at least one-quarter (26 percent - 33 percent) of the ASRS reports of pilots entering, crossing, taking, or otherwise transgressing the runway. While the FAA Advisory Circular on flightcrew surface operations (FAA, 2003) recommends that only one flightcrew member perform heads-down tasks while the aircraft is taxiing, this analysis suggests that even that may be problematic. **The most effective pilot mitigation strategy that can be implemented immediately is to minimize heads-down activity during taxi.** Ideally, checklists and system programming would never be performed while the aircraft is in motion as heads-down activity distracts the pilot from realizing the proximity to the runway.

Continue to Maintain Improvements in Airport Signs and Markings. Pilots cited poor signage and ambiguous surface markings as contributing factors in some incidents. Since the dates of these incidents, progress has been made in improving airport signs and marking. Renewed attention has been given to refreshing faded hold-short lines and replacing absent, poorly visible, and ambiguous signs.

Augment Pilot's Expectation of the Hold-short Lines. Pilots often reported that they failed to hold short of a runway because the hold-short lines were placed in an unexpected location. This situation could be helped by using anticipatory markings to signal to the pilot that they are approaching a runway. Highlighting the center taxi line near the hold-short lines has been proven (in a pilot program at PVD airport) to help alert pilots that they are approaching the hold lines. These enhanced marking are planned for more widespread implementation and are expected to help reduce the incidence of pilots inadvertently crossing the hold-short lines.

Examine the potential risks and benefits of changing "Taxi Into Position and Hold" to "Line up and Wait." Standard International Civil Aviation Organization (ICAO) phraseology for "taxi into position and hold" is "line up and wait." While the instruction to "taxi into position and hold" is not in itself problematic in the U.S, confusion can arise when controllers issue non-standard instructions such as "taxi to the number one position and hold short." Also, from a human factors standpoint, "line up and wait" is preferable since it is does not contain any words similar to (and thus confusable with) "hold short." The FAA is currently assessing whether or not there is a safety case for changing the wording of this instruction. The results of this analysis point to the importance of this effort.

Continue to Monitor Risks of Using "Taxi To" Instructions. Instructions to "taxi to" a location (such as a departure runway) include a clearance to cross all intervening runways. Implied clearances to cross runways have contributed to runway incursions in which the aircraft was in a different location than either the controller or the pilot thought. The FAA has examined incursions to determine the relative risk involved in issuing "taxi to" instructions that include a clearance to cross intervening runways. To date, the numbers of incursions that involved "taxi to" instructions has been too few to demonstrate an unacceptable level of risk. The results of this study suggest that continued monitoring of the risks and benefits of using multiple crossing clearances with "taxi to" instructions is merited.

4. References

Cardosi, K., Falzarano, P., and Han, S. (1998). *Pilot-Controller Communication Errors: An Analysis of Aviation Safety Reporting System (ASRS) Reports.* DOT/FAA/AR-98/17.

Cardosi, K. and Yost, A. (2001). *Controller and Pilot Error in Airport Operations: A Review of Previous Research and Analysis of Safety Data.* DOT/FAA/AR-00/51.

Federal Aviation Administration (2003). *Flightcrew procedures during taxi operations.* FAA Advisory Circular # AC 120-74 A.

Federal Aviation Administration. (2005). *FAA Runway Safety Report: Runway Incursion Trends and Initiatives at Towered Airports in the United States, FY 2001 and FY 2004.* Air Traffic Safety Services.

Appendix A. Airport Identifiers

ATL	THE WILLIAM B. HARTSFIELD ATLANTA INTL, GA
BOS	GENERAL EDWARD LAWRENCE LOGAN INTL, MA
BWI	BALTIMORE-WASHINGTON INTL, MD
CLE	CLEVELAND-HOPKINS INTL, OH
CLT	CHARLOTTE/DOUGLAS INTL, NC
CVG	CINCINNATI/NORTHERN KENTUCKY INTL, KY
DCA	RONALD REAGAN WASHINGTON NATIONAL, DC
DEN	DEN - DENVER INTL, CO
DFW	DALLAS-FORT WORTH INTL, TX
DTW	DETROIT METROPOLITAN WAYNE COUNTY, MI
EWR	NEWARK INTL, NJ
HNL	HONOLULU INTL, HI
IAD	WASHINGTON DULLES INTL, DC
IAH	GEORGE BUSH INTERCONTINENTAL AIRPORT/HOUSTON, TX
JFK	JOHN F. KENNEDY INTL, NY
LAS	MCCARRAN INTL, NV
LAX	LOS ANGELES INTL, CA
LGA	LA GUARDIA, NY
MCO	ORLANDO INTL, FL
MDW	CHICAGO MIDWAY, IL
MEM	MEMPHIS INTL, TN
MIA	MIAMI INTL, FL
MSP	MINNEAPOLIS-ST PAUL INTL (WOLD-CHAMBERLAIN), MN
ORD	CHICAGO-O'HARE INTL, IL
PHL	PHILADELPHIA INTL, PA
PHX	PHOENIX SKY HARBOR INTL, AZ
PIT	GEORGE BUSH INTERCONTINENTAL AIRPORT/HOUSTON, TX
SEA	SEATTLE-TACOMA INTL, WA
SFO	SAN FRANCISCO INTL, CA
SLC	SALT LAKE CITY INTL, UT
SNA	JOHN WAYNE AIRPORT-ORANGE COUNTY, CA
STL	LAMBERT-ST. LOUIS INTL, MO
TEB	TETERBORO, NJ
TPA	TAMPA INTL, FL

Appendix B. Factor Taxonomy

Communications Factors
    Pilot Factors
        Readback Error
        Pilot used improper phraseology
        Pilot confused by standard ATC phraseology
        Pilot misunderstood the clearance
        Pilot accepted clearance intended for another aircraft
        Pilot failed to clarify ambiguous instruction/situation
        Similar callsigns on the same frequency
        Pilot monitoring the wrong or multiple frequencies
    ATC Factors
        Hearback Errors - Controller failed to correct error in pilot's readback (Type I)
        Hearback Error Type II – Controller failed to detect the discrepancy between the
            correct readback and the intended instruction
        Pilot reported that ATC used non-standard phraseology
        Pilot reported that ATC used the wrong, or omitted, taxiway or runway designator
        Pilot reported that ATC issued instruction too late for aircraft to comply
        Pilot reported that ATC issued conflicting clearances to two or more aircraft
        Pilot confused by instructions
        Pilot reported that ATC speech rate and/or quality of speech was a factor
    Frequency/Equipment Issues
        Frequency Congestion
        Blocked/stepped-on transmissions
        Poor Radio Quality
Airport Surface Issues
    Non-standard hold-short markings
    Hold-short lines were faded or difficult to see
    Lack of markings or signs (other than hold-short lines)
    Inadequate or missing lights
    Complex intersection of runways and/or taxiways
    Closely spaced parallel runways
    Construction activity
Position Awareness
    Pilot performing "heads-down" duties
        Aircraft equipment issues
        Programming the flight management system
        Map or chart reading
        Checklists
    Airport diagram issue
    Misidentified location
    Unfamiliarity with airport or route
    Speed of Aircraft

Automatic Processing Factors
      Reverting to habit
      Following another aircraft beyond the point of clearance
      Pilot expectation of a particular clearance
      Pilot expectation of the location of hold-short lines
Environmental Factors
      Night conditions
      Wet or icy runway/taxiway
      Restricted visibility
      Wind
      IMC or marginal conditions
Other Human Performance Issues
      Fatigue
      Cockpit distraction
      Distraction outside the cockpit
      Distracted by previous events
      Rushed due to schedule pressure
      Rushed due to ATC urgency